FOCUS ON

ELEMENTARY

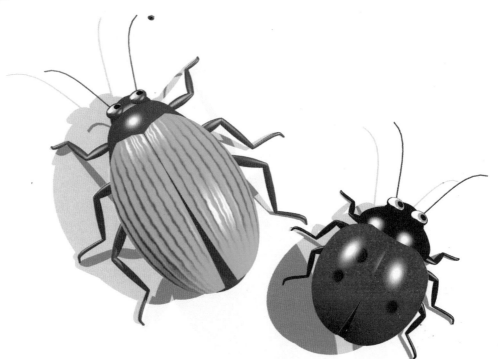

Rebecca W. Keller, PhD

Cover design: David Keller
Opening page illustrations: David Keller
Text illustrations: Janet Moneymaker, Rebecca W. Keller, PhD

Focus On Elementary Biology Student Textbook (softcover)
ISBN # 978-1-936114-50-4

Published by Gravitas Publications, Inc.
www.gravitaspublications.com

GRAVITAS
PUBLICATIONS

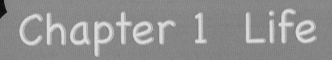

Chapter 1 Life

1.1 Studying Life

What makes plants, dogs, and beetles different from rocks, dirt, and metal? Maybe you have noticed that rocks don't move like dogs, and that dirt doesn't need food, like plants. Maybe you have seen that forks and knives, made of metals, don't crawl around in the kitchen, like beetles. Living things are different from rocks, and dirt, and metals because living things are alive.

What does it mean to be alive? Think about how you are different from a rock. You need food and a rock doesn't. One feature of being alive is needing food.

Second, you can walk, run, jump, curl up into a ball, and roll on the carpet. But a rock can't move. So, another feature of being alive is the ability to move.

Finally, a rock can't make baby rocks, but plants, animals, and humans all make baby plants or baby animals or baby humans. So another feature of being alive is the ability to reproduce.

As we can see, living things are much different from non-living things.

1.2 Sorting Living Things

How do we keep track of all of the living things we find on the planet? Is there a way to sort them? Why would we want to sort them?

Sorting living things helps us understand how they are different and how they are the same. For example, what if you had some yellow blocks and some blue blocks? How would you sort them?

HOW WOULD YOU SORT THE BLOCKS?

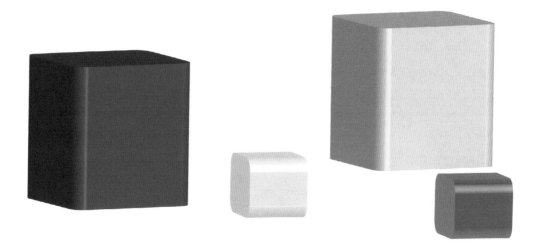

If you sort your blocks according to color, you can see that the blue blocks are different from the yellow blocks. However, you might also notice that some of the blue blocks are the same size as some of the yellow blocks. So you could also sort them by size. By sorting, you can see how some blocks are different (different color), but also how some are the same (same size).

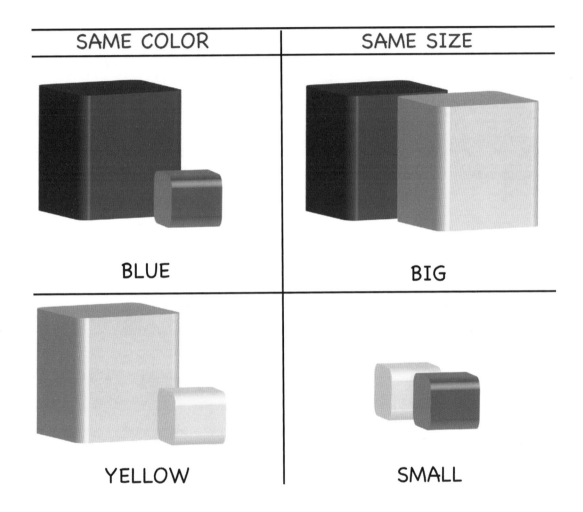

SAME COLOR	SAME SIZE
BLUE	BIG
YELLOW	SMALL

A very long time ago a man named Carolus Linnaeus thought about how to sort living things. He came up with a system of sorting all of the creatures on the planet. We call this system taxonomy.

Taxonomy is a branch of biology that is concerned with how to sort living things.

We sort living things by looking at their different features.

A feature is anything like hair, hooves, feathers, or green leaves.

For example, we might sort animals that have hair from animals that don't have hair. We might sort plants that live in the soil from plants that live in the water.

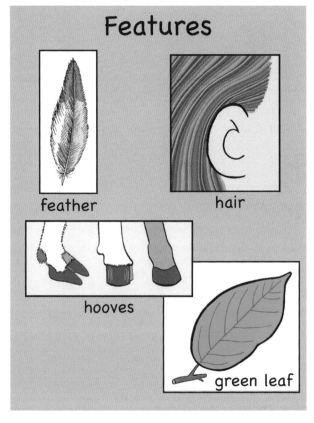

Features

feather

hair

hooves

green leaf

We might also sort very small creatures that we can't even see from larger creatures that we can see. Looking at the features of living things helps us sort them.

1.3 Domains and Kingdoms

It is very difficult to decide how to sort living things—there are so many different features! Once upon a time, living things were sorted into only two large groups: plants and animals. However, as scientists learned more about all of the different creatures, they had to make more groups.

Today, scientists use three large groups to sort living things. These groups are called domains. The names of the domains are Eukarya, Bacteria, and Archaea. These domains are then further divided into six kingdoms which are Plantae, Animalia, Protista, Fungi, Bacteria, and Archaea.

House plants are in the kingdom Plantae

The kingdom Plantae groups all of the plants. Houseplants are in the kingdom Plantae.

Dogs are in the kingdom
Animalia

Animalia groups all of the animals. Dogs are in the kingdom Animalia. So are cats, frogs, and butterflies.

Bacteria and Archaea are kingdoms that group some of the very small creatures that we can't see when using only our eyes.

Protista is a group for very small creatures called protists.

And finally, Fungi groups things like toadstools and mushrooms.

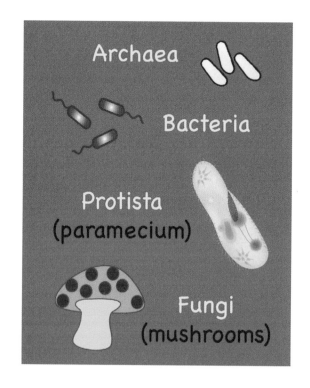

1.4 Sorting Within Kingdoms

Scientists first sort living things into their domains and then sort them into their kingdoms. Then scientists organize the living things into smaller groups to better understand them. So, living things in different domains are sorted into kingdoms and then further sorted into smaller, different groups.

To sort living things into smaller groups, scientists again look for different or similar features. For example, both birds and cats are animals, but we can see that birds are different from cats. For one thing, birds have wings and fly, but cats don't fly. Cats have fur and eat birds.

Even though birds and cats are both animals, they are different from each other. All of the birds are put into a group for birds, and all of the cats are put into a group for cats.

What about tigers and house cats? They are both cats. Are they exactly the same? In fact, they aren't. Even though tigers and house cats have some similar features, they are also different. For example, house cats don't usually eat their owners, but tigers could! So house cats and tigers are put into even smaller groups within the larger grouping of "cats."

1.5 Naming

How do we name all of the creatures we find? Because there are so many different languages, and because there are so many different living things, scientists use a scientific name to name each living thing. Every plant and animal, fungus, bacterium, and archaeon has a scientific name. The scientific name for each living thing comes from the Latin language. Each creature has two Latin names. The first name is called the genus and the second name is called the species.

The Latin name for a house cat is *Felis catus* and the Latin name for humans is *Homo sapiens* which means "man wise."

1.6 Summary

○ Living things are different from non-living things. All living things need food and can reproduce, and some living things can move.

○ Scientists sort living things into groups to understand them better.

○ Domains and kingdoms are two kinds of groups that scientists use to sort living things.

○ All living things have a special scientific name which is in Latin.

Chapter 2 Cells: A Tiny City

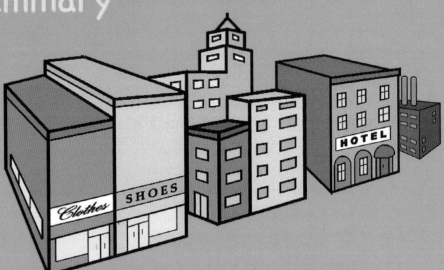

2.1 Creatures

Have you ever wondered what makes a frog a frog or a rose a rose? Have you ever wondered what you are made of?

We saw in Chapter 1 that living things are different from non-living things. But what are living things made of?

We know from chemistry that both living and non-living things are made of atoms. We also know from chemistry that atoms fit together to make molecules. But how do molecules fit together to make living things live?

2.2 The Cell

The atoms and molecules in living things are designed to fit together in special ways to make cells. The atoms and molecules inside cells are very small, so you can't see them. But when they are put together they make up the cell.

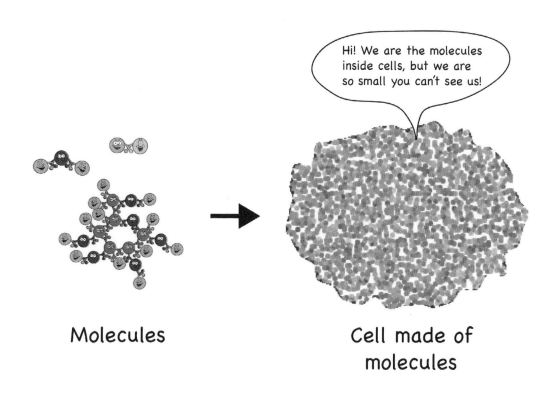

Hi! We are the molecules inside cells, but we are so small you can't see us!

Molecules

Cell made of molecules

Cells are designed to fit together in special ways to make all of the parts of living things. For example, molecules fit together to make skin cells, and skin cells fit together to make skin.

Molecules also fit together to make muscle cells, and muscle cells fit together to make muscles.

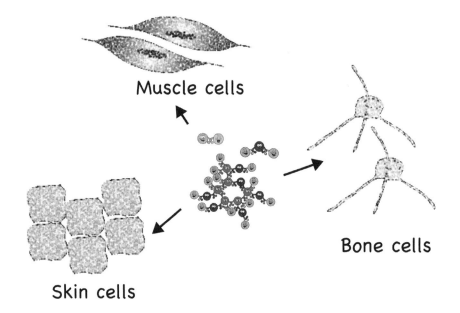

Muscle cells

Bone cells

Skin cells

Bone cells, muscle cells, and skin cells fit together to make arms or legs or fingers.

2.3 A Tiny City

Cells are like tiny cities. Imagine what it takes to make even one item we use in a city—like milk. What does it take to make milk?

We know that milk comes from cows. Cows are not usually in the city, but in the country, so we have to go to the country to get the milk from the cows.

Once we have the milk, we have to move it to the city. We need a big truck to move the milk.

But it can't be just any kind of truck, it has to be a special truck that can move the milk. If it were a sand truck, we might get sand in our milk. So we must use a milk truck.

Once the milk is in the city, what happens to it? First the milk is put into cartons. It would be hard to get our milk directly from the milk truck, so we need to put the milk into cartons.

Once the milk is put into cartons, we have to put it somewhere we can find it, like a grocery store. Once

it is in the grocery store, your mom or dad can buy it and put it on the table!

Think about all of the people it takes to bring milk to your table. We need people to milk the cows, clean the raw milk so we can drink it, move the milk to the truck, drive the truck into town, put the milk into cartons, and finally, put the milk in the grocery store so your mom and dad can buy the milk.

It takes a lot of people to perform all those tasks! And they have to all be done in the right order.

Imagine what would happen if the milk was put into cartons in the wrong order. What do you think would happen if the cartons were sealed before the milk was put in?

The process for making milk is similar to how a cell works. There are lots of proteins doing all kinds of jobs inside a cell that keep the cell alive.

Each job has to be done by a special protein, and all the jobs have to be done in a particular way and in a particular order.

The cell is like an amazing little city doing amazing little tasks all together to keep living things living.

2.4 Parts of a Cell

Cells have lots of different parts like cities have lots of different places. We have talked about how cities provide milk, but there are also other places in cities that provide other things.

For example, there is usually a downtown area in the city that has many important places, like the courthouse or the tax department. Scattered through the city are post offices where letters are mailed back and forth, grocery stores for buying milk, hotels for people who visit, and factories for making things.

There are lots of different places and lots of people doing lots of different jobs.

Nucleus (building)

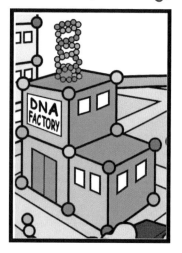

Cells are like cities in this way. In most cells there is a central part that does many of the important jobs in the cell. This central part is called the nucleus. The nucleus of human and plant cells holds all of the important information, called DNA, for the cell.

Golgi Apparatus (building)
Ribosomes (protein man)

Outside the nucleus there are lots of places that do special jobs inside the cell. There is a place called the golgi apparatus which makes proteins. There are also special proteins called ribosomes that make other proteins.

Kinesin (truck)
Microtubules (road)

There are "roads," called microtubules, that move proteins from place to place. And there are "trucks" called kinesin that carry the proteins on the "roads."

Putting it all together, the cell seems a lot like a little city, with every protein and molecule doing its part!

A City Cell

2.5 Summary

○ Atoms and molecules fit together to make cells.

○ Cells fit together in special ways to make the parts of living things.

○ All the parts of a cell have special jobs.

Chapter 3 Food for Plants

3.1 Introduction

How do plants eat? Do they eat spaghetti or french fries? Have you ever met a plant at the diner drinking a milk shake?

No, probably not. Plants can't eat spaghetti or french fries or drink milk shakes.

In fact, most plants have to make their own food. They make their food using sunlight.

3.2 Factories

As we saw in Chapter 2, cells are like little cities. Just like cities have factories that make milk or cereal, cells also have places inside them that act like factories.

We call these little factories organelles. An organelle is like a little organ inside cells that does a special job.

A food factory (called a chloroplast) is a kind of organelle.

There are many different kinds of organelles inside cells. To make food, a plant cell has a food factory (or organelle) called a chloroplast.

Part of the chloroplast that catches sunlight (chlorphyll molecule)

3.3 How Plants Make Food

Plants use sunlight to make food. This process is called photosynthesis. Photo means "light" and synthesis means "to make." So photosynthesis means "to make with light."

Plants do this by catching the light from the Sun in a very special molecule inside their cells. This molecule is called chlorophyll. The job of the chlorophyll molecule is to catch sunlight and use it to make sugar!

3.4 Food Factories

Food for a plant is made in all of the green parts of the plant. This is because the chloroplasts are found in all these green parts. Green plant leaves and green plant stems both have chloroplasts.

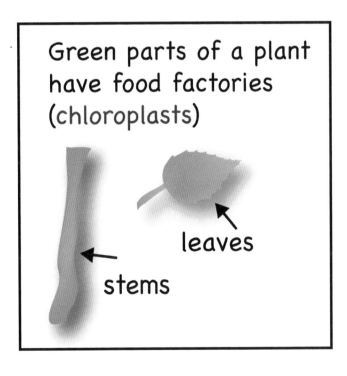

Green parts of a plant have food factories (chloroplasts)

leaves

stems

The green color in a chloroplast comes from the chlorophyll molecule. The chlorophyll molecule catches the sunlight and also makes the leaf or stem green.

3.5 Different Leaves

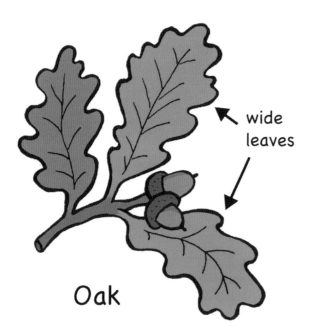

Oak

There are many different kinds of leaves on plants and trees. Some trees, like oak trees, have very wide leaves. This is so they can collect as much sunlight as possible.

Other trees, like a willow tree, have lots of narrow leaves. Having lots of leaves will also help a tree collect as much sunlight as possible.

Black Willow

What happens to leaves when they change color? Why do leaves turn yellow in autumn and then fall off in winter? Leaves change color in autumn because in autumn the days are shorter.

It is a lot of work for a tree to use sunlight to make sugar to use for food, so when there isn't enough sunlight to do this, the tree gets rid of its leaves. A tree knows when the days are getting shorter, and this causes the green chlorophyll molecules to go away, the tree to stop making food, and the leaves to first turn color and then fall off.

3.6 Summary

○ Most plants make their own food by photosynthesis.

○ Plants have tiny factories called chloroplasts inside their cells for making food.

○ The green parts of a plant, like leaves and stems, make the food.

○ Leaves change color in autumn when the tree doesn't have enough sunlight to make food.

Chapter 4 Plant Parts

4.1 Introduction

Many plants live and grow in soil and above the soil—in the air. The part of the plant that lives in the soil is the root. The parts of the plant that live in the air are the leaf, stem and flower. These different parts of a plant are called organs.

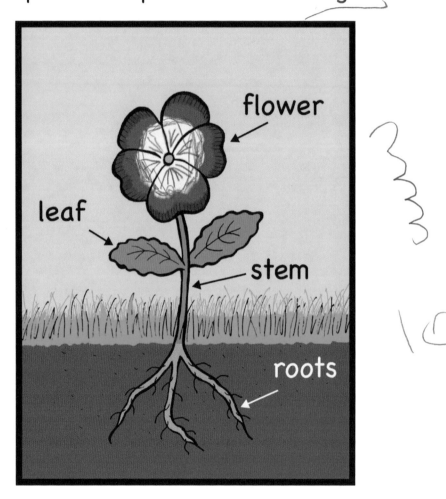

Plants get what they need to live and grow from below the ground (the soil), and from above the ground (sunlight and air.)

4.2 Below the Ground: The Roots

Plants cannot walk around or fly to go get their food, like insects or other animals do. Instead, plants have roots in the dirt. The roots take things from the soil that the plant uses to make food.

Soil has some of the nutrients plants need to make food. The soil also holds the water that plants need in order to grow.

Roots also help keep plants from getting tossed around by wind or bad weather. Plants help keep the soil from blowing away.

4.3 Above the Soil: Leaves, Stems, Flowers

Above the soil, we find the leaves and stem. We saw in Chapter 3 that the leaves and stem of a plant take in the Sun's energy to make food. The Sun gives plants energy to make food.

For flowering plants, the flower is also above the soil. The flower is the part of the plant that turns into the fruit. The fruit holds seeds for new plants.

4.4 Other Places Plants Live

Plants can also live in oceans. There are different kinds of plants that live in oceans. Some plants are very tiny, like plant plankton. Plant plankton provide food for the animals in the ocean. Most plant plankton are microscopic, meaning you can only see them with a microscope.

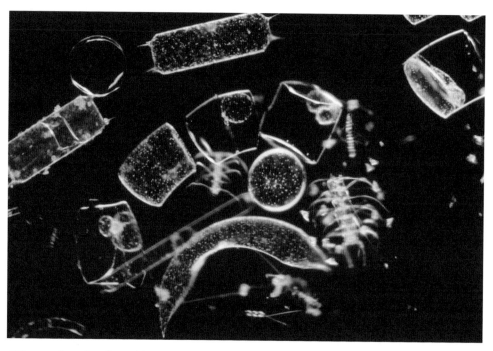

Tiny plants (so tiny you need a microscope to see them) called plant plankton are found in the ocean.

Chris Parks/imagequestmarine.com

Other ocean plants can be very large, like kelp. Kelp is a type of seaweed and can be several yards long. Seaweed can be red, brown, or green.

Like land plants, ocean plants need sunlight to make food. So most ocean plants are found close enough to the surface that they can get sunlight.

4.5 Summary

- Plants have different organs that help them live and grow.

- Below the ground, the roots help the plant get nutrients and water from the soil to make food.

- Above the soil, the leaves and stem help the plant take in sunlight to make food.

- The flowers are also above the soil. The flowers turn into fruit which hold the seeds for new plants.

Chapter 5 Growing a Plant

5.1 The Beginning: Seeds

Plants grow from seeds. Seeds can be lots of different shapes and sizes. A seed can be tiny or large, blue or brown, round or skinny.

Inside a seed there is a tiny plant called an embryo.

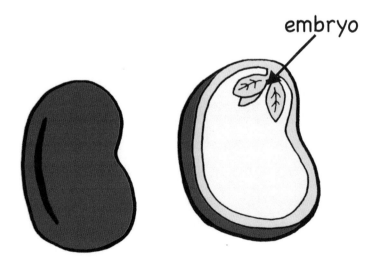

If a seed gets planted in the soil and if there is enough water, the embryo will start to grow. The water will make the inside of the seed swell, and the little embryo will break out of the seed and grow into a baby plant.

5.2 The Middle: Baby Plants

Once the embryo breaks out of the seed, it starts to grow. As it grows, it will change from an embryo to a seedling. A baby plant is called a seedling.

As the seedling grows, it will push its roots down into the soil so that it can get water. It will also start to grow leaves so that it can get sunlight to make food. The sunlight will help the seedling straighten out and grow into a big plant.

5.3 The Finish: Flowers and Fruit

Once the plant is fully grown, it will want to make baby plants. There are different kinds of plants and different ways plants make baby plants.

One kind of plant is called a flowering plant. A flowering plant produces flowers. The flowers produce fruit, and the fruit hold the seeds.

5.4 Starting Again: The Life Cycle

When the baby plant has grown into a big plant, and when the big plant grows the flowers, and when a flower makes the fruit, and when the fruit drops the seed—a new baby plant can grow. This is called a life cycle. A cycle is something that repeats itself. So a life cycle is how life repeats itself.

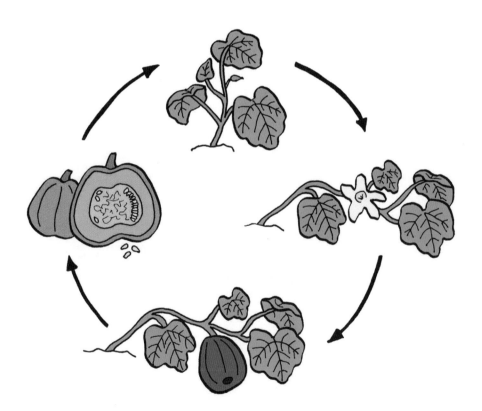

It takes a flowering plant to make a seed of a flowering plant. And it takes a seed of a flowering plant to make a flowering plant. This is how flowering plants make new flowering plants.

5.5 Summary

○ Plants grow from seeds.

○ Inside a seed is a tiny plant called an embryo.

○ A baby plant is called a seedling.

○ A flowering plant produces flowers that make fruit that hold the seeds for new plants.

Chapter 6 Protists

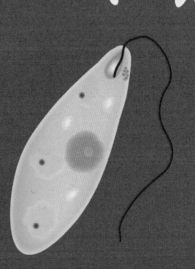

6.1 Tiny Creatures

How tiny is the smallest living creature? If you look at yourself, you might think you are pretty small compared to your dad, but are you the smallest living creature? No! You are not as small as your cat. The cat is smaller than you are. But is a cat the smallest living thing? No. In fact the cat chases (and sometimes eats) moths or birds or mice that are smaller than the cat.

How about a moth? Do you think the moth is the smallest living creature?

No, a ladybug is smaller than a moth and an ant is smaller than a ladybug, and a gnat is even smaller than an ant. So how small is the smallest living creature?

The smallest living creatures are so small that you can't even see them when using just your eyes. There is a whole world of small creatures that live in ponds, in oceans, in dirt, and even inside of you that you can't see!

One type of small creature you can't see with only your eyes is called a protist (also called a protozoan). A protist is a small creature that can do many of the things bigger creatures (like you) do. Protists can crawl and swim and eat and sense light. Protists are very small, but can do amazing things.

6.2 How Can We See Them?

If protists are so small, how can we see them? Scientists use a microscope to see small creatures like protists. A microscope is a special kind of tool that helps you look at things too small for your eyes alone to see.

You have probably used a tool called a magnifying glass to see small things. For example, if you leave your pie outside you might discover in the morning that ants have come to have a taste. You can see the ants with your eyes, but if you use a magnifying glass, you can see them even more clearly. They

look big in the
magnifying glass,
and you can
see the hair on
their legs, the
smoothness of
their backs, and
the number of
pie crumbs they
are taking.

A microscope is
like a magnifying glass in that it makes very small
things look big. A microscope has a lens, usually
made of glass. The lens magnifies (makes whatever

Microscope

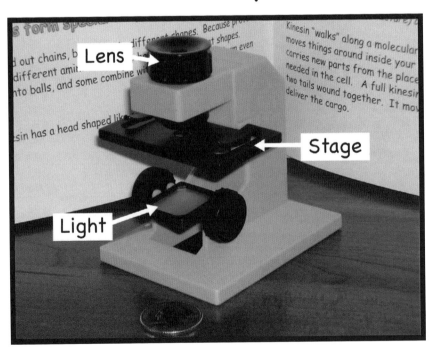

you are seeing look bigger) like the magnifying glass. But a microscope is also different from a magnifying glass. For example, a microscope has a stage where you put the sample. The stage helps keep the sample still, and the sample is the thing you want to see—like pond water or ocean water. Also, a microscope usually has a little light that makes the sample brighter. In some microscopes, the light is a little mirror that captures room light and reflects it back through the microscope.

The first person to see protists was a man named Anton van Leeuwenhoek. He was from Holland, and with his microscope he saw little animals in pond water. He also found them in his mouth!

6.3 Different Kinds of Tiny Creatures

There are many different kinds of protists that can be seen only with a microscope. But how do you know what kinds of creatures you are seeing?

We saw in Chapter 1 that when scientists sort living things into groups, they are easier to study. The kingdom protista is a very large group with over sixty thousand different kinds of protists. Because it is such a large group, scientists need to sort the protists into even smaller groups.

One way to sort protists into smaller groups is to notice the different ways protists move. There are three ways that protists move.

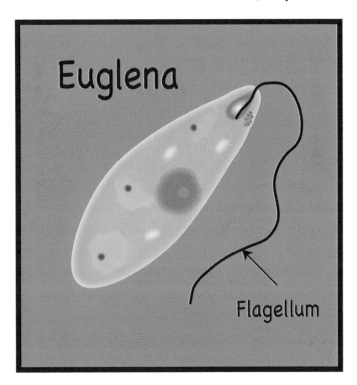

Euglena

Flagellum

One way protists move is to swim with a big tail called a flagellum. Some protists, like Euglena, have a flagellum.

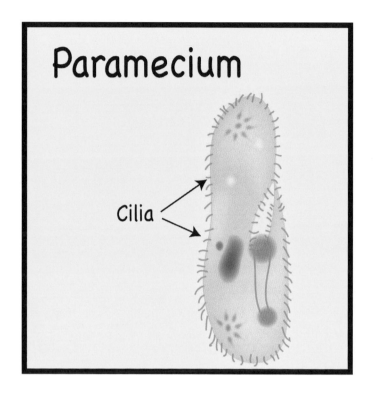

Paramecium

Cilia

Another way protists move is by using small hair-like features called cilia. Cilia beat fast in the water making the protists move forwards and backwards and sideways. A paramecium uses cilia to move.

Finally, some protists crawl. Amoebas are protists that use false feet called pseudopods to crawl from one place to another.

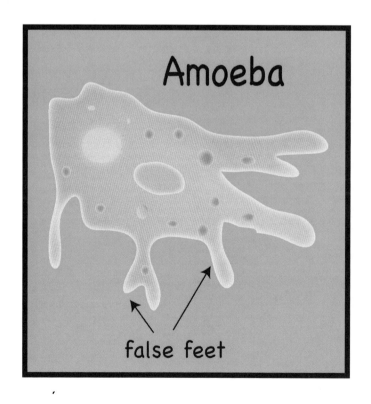

Amoeba

false feet

6.4 Summary

○ There are many small creatures that we cannot see with our eyes.

○ Scientists use a microscope to see small creatures.

○ Protists are small creatures that can be found in pond water and ocean water.

○ One way scientists sort protists is by how they move.

○ Protists move by using a flagellum, by using cilia, or by crawling using pseudopods (false feet).

Chapter 7 Protists Eat

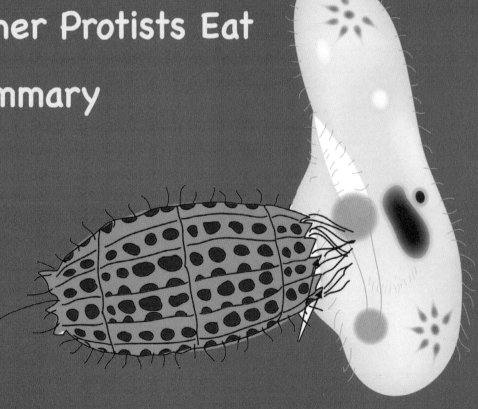

7.1 Euglena Eat

A euglena uses sunlight to make its own food like a plant does. A euglena is not a plant, but it has chloroplasts just like a plant. Remember from Chapter 3 that chloroplasts are special parts inside plant cells that collect sunlight. The chloroplast contains chlorophyll which captures the sunlight. Chlorophyll also makes a plant green, and since euglena have chlorophyll, euglena are also green.

The euglena will swim toward the sunlight so that it can make food. A euglena has a little eyespot that helps it know where to find the sunlight.

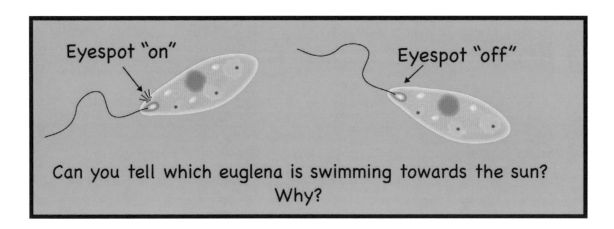

Eyespot "on"

Eyespot "off"

Can you tell which euglena is swimming towards the sun?
Why?

7.2 Paramecia Eat

Not all protists can make their own food like a euglena does. A paramecium has to go find its food, just like we do, but a paramecium cannot go to the grocery store for eggs and milk like we can. It must swim around with its cilia to look for food in the water.

A paramecium eats other small creatures, like bacteria or algae. The paramecium has a mouth that it uses to capture food. The mouth does not move like a human mouth and it doesn't have any teeth. The cilia around the mouth move, or beat, rapidly and this makes the water near the mouth of the paramecium swirl. Take your hands and move them in some water, and you can feel the water swirling around your hands. A paramecium uses the swirling water to move food toward its mouth.

When the food enters the mouth of the paramecium, it travels through a small tube into a tiny stomach and gets digested. The paramecium takes what it needs from the digested food, and the unused food is pushed out through a small hole.

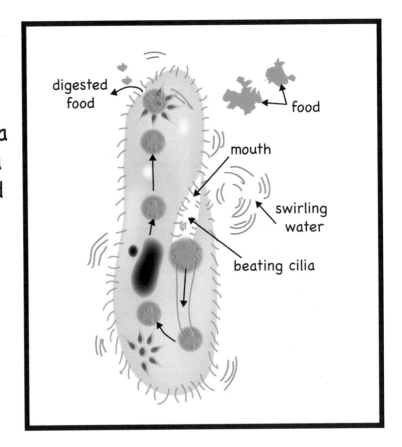

Although a paramecium has only one cell, it can move, eat, and digest food just like larger creatures. The paramecium is an amazing creature for being so small.

7.3 Amoebas Eat

An amoeba eats with its feet! Can you imagine eating with your feet? It would be pretty hard for you to eat with your feet, but not for an amoeba.

An amoeba uses its false feet, or pseudopods, to surround the food it wants to eat. Once the food is surrounded, the amoeba brings its feet together and makes something like a stomach out of the false feet that surround the food.

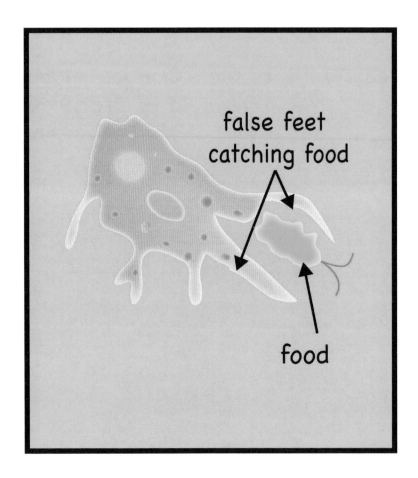

false feet catching food

food

The stomach then absorbs the food into the body of the amoeba. That is how the amoeba eats with its feet!

7.4 Other Protists Eat

There are other protists that eat in other ways. For example a protist called a *Coleps* rotates its whole body to swim through the water.

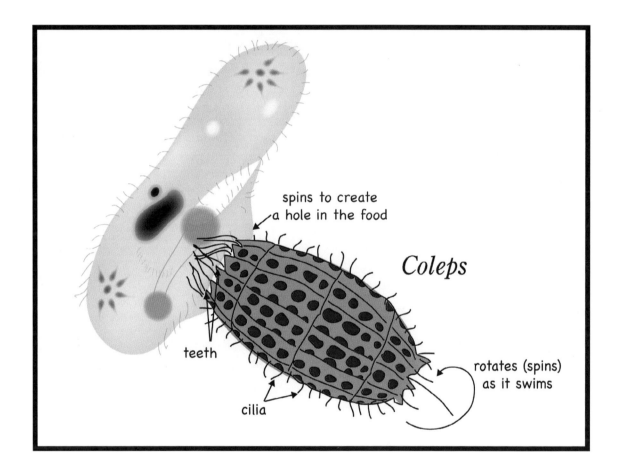

It also rotates as it eats. As it rotates, it uses its sharp teeth to bore through the food like a tiny drill. Then it eats the food it removes from the hole it has made with its teeth.

7.5 Summary

○ A euglena uses chloroplasts, like a plant, to make its food.

○ A paramecium uses cilia to swirl the water and sweep food into its mouth.

○ An ameoba uses its pseudopods, or false feet, to capture food and eat.

○ Other protists use other ways to eat.

Chapter 8 Butterflies

8.1 Beautiful Butterflies

If you go outside on a warm summer day, you might see a butterfly. Butterflies are insects found during the spring and summer months. They often have beautifully colored wings and fly from flower to flower looking for nectar.

If you look closely at the butterfly, you might see tiny scales on its wings. Butterflies belong to a group of insects called Lepidoptera. All of the insects in this group have scales on their wings.

8.2 The Beginning: Eggs

Have you ever wondered how a butterfly begins life? Just like other living things, a butterfly begins life as an egg. When the time is right, the mother butterfly will lay some eggs. Butterfly eggs are usually very small, and they all look different. Some are fuzzy, and some have ridges. Some are white and round, and some are thin and orange.

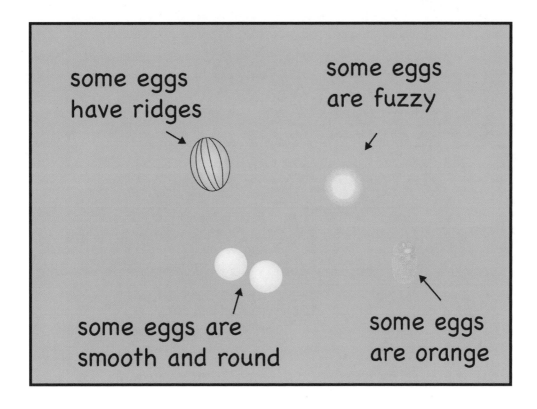

Butterfly eggs can be hard to see, but if you look carefully you might find one! But where do you look?

The mother butterfly tries to find a safe place to lay her eggs. She looks for a place where the eggs will have food when they hatch.

She looks for a place that will be warm and dry and protected from other bugs. So the mother butterfly will usually glue the eggs to the back of a green leaf. The leaf protects the eggs and can also be used for food when the eggs hatch.

8.3 The Middle: Caterpillar

When an egg is ready to hatch, a caterpillar is born. The caterpillar comes out of the egg, and the very first thing it does is eat! In fact, eating is about all the caterpillar does! It eats and eats and eats. Most caterpillars eat plants, but a few will eat other insects. The main job of the caterpillar is to eat enough food so that, when the time is right, it will be ready to become a butterfly.

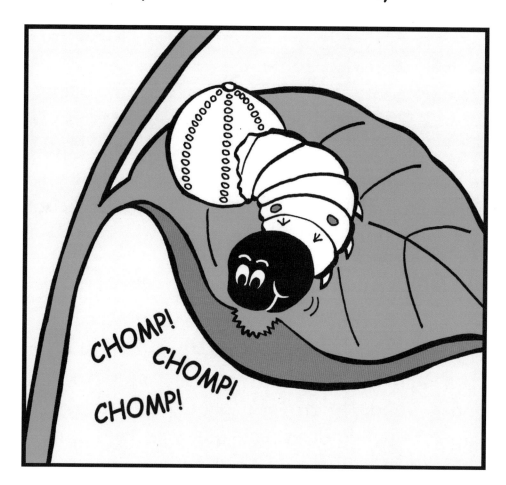

Caterpillars come in all different colors, sizes, and textures. Some are green, and some are brown.

Some are smooth, and some are furry. Some are very small, and some grow big and fat! Some even have lots of stripes of pretty colors. There are many different kinds of caterpillars that turn into many different types of butterflies.

As the caterpillar grows, its skin stays the same size. So, several times while the caterpillar is growing, it will molt, or shed its too small skin, and form new skin. Once the caterpillar has eaten all the food it needs to eat and grown as big as it needs to grow, it finds a nice place to rest before becoming a butterfly.

8.4 The Change: Chrysalis

The caterpillar looks and looks for a nice place to stay while it turns into a butterfly. It will look for leaves or the undersides of ledges or tree limbs. When it finds a good place to stop, it attaches itself to the underside of the leaf or ledge with a small button of silk. Then it sheds its skin for the last time. The new skin becomes the hard shell of the chrysalis.

A chrysalis is like a cozy house that keeps the caterpillar warm and dry. Some chrysalises cover the whole caterpillar and are very thick and tough. But other chrysalises are thinner, and you can see the caterpillar underneath.

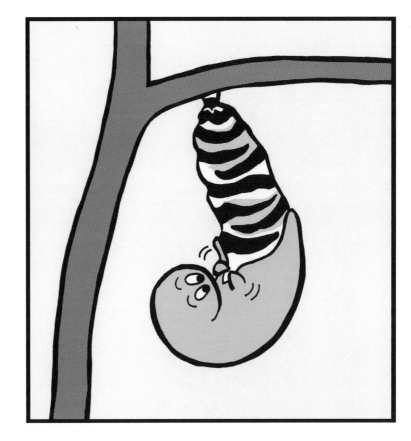

Inside the chrysalis the caterpillar changes into a butterfly. The body of the caterpillar starts to change, and wings begin to grow. The long feet of the butterfly grow, and tentacles begin to show.

When the caterpillar has completely changed, or transformed, it is ready to emerge from the chrysalis as a butterfly.

8.5 The End: Adult Butterfly

When the butterfly is ready to come out, a hole forms in the chrysalis. The butterfly must wriggle through the hole to get out. It looks like the butterfly struggles, but the tiny hole actually helps the wings of the butterfly get ready to be used for flying.

Once the butterfly has emerged from the chrysalis, it takes a moment to spread its new wings. The wings continue to expand as water from the body is removed. In a few hours the butterfly is ready, and it spreads its wings and flies away!

The adult butterfly eats nectar from flowers and sometimes even travels far distances. When the adult butterfly is ready, it will lay new eggs, starting the life cycle for a new butterfly all over again!

8.6 Summary

- Butterflies are insects that have scales on their wings.
- A butterfly begins life as a tiny egg.
- The mother butterfly lays her eggs on the backs of leaves.
- A caterpillar emerges from the egg, and its job is to eat!
- The caterpillar makes a chrysalis to protect it while it changes into a butterfly.

Chapter 9 Frogs

9.1 Life on Land and in Water

Have you ever thought about what it must be like to live both on the land and in the water? Imagine going for a stroll in the park and then having tea with the fish in the pond. It might be fun!

Think about what you might need to have to be able to live on both the land and in the water. What kind of skin would you need? What kind of lungs would you need? What about your feet? What kind of feet would you need?

Frogs are creatures that live both on the land and in the water. Frogs have special skin, lungs, and feet that are designed to live both on the land and in the water.

Frogs are called amphibians. The word amphibian means "both lives" because frogs live two lives. One life they live is on the land, and the other life they live is in the water.

9.2 The Beginning: Eggs

A frog begins its life in the water as an egg. You probably know that a chicken also starts out as an egg. When you look at a chicken egg you can see that it has a yellow yolk in the middle and a hard outer shell.

A frog egg is much smaller than a chicken egg, but it is not too small to see. If you look closely, you can see that a frog egg also has a yolk. But the yolk of a frog egg is not yellow like a chicken egg. Instead, it is usually black or gray or even black and white.

A frog egg is not covered in a hard outer shell like a chicken egg, but sits in a clump of goo. The goo looks like clear Jell-O. This goo is sticky and

helps the eggs stay attached to plants or logs in the water where the mother frog puts them. The goo also helps keep the eggs safe and stuck together so that they don't get lost.

9.3 The Middle: Tadpoles

Once the mother frog lays the eggs, she swims away. The eggs hatch on their own. It takes anywhere from a few days to several weeks for the frog eggs to hatch. When they are ready to hatch, little tadpoles emerge from the eggs in the goo. The

tadpoles eat the goo for food until they get a little bigger.

Newly born tadpoles are small and fragile. They stick themselves to strands of grass until they get stronger. Tadpoles have gills that help them breath under water and tails that help them swim. Once they grow a little bigger, they swim around eating algae until they are ready to turn into frogs.

9.4 The Change: Tadpoles to Frogs

After the tadpole has been swimming and eating and growing, it is ready to become a frog. Unlike a butterfly, a tadpole does not need to be in a chrysalis while it is making the change into a frog. It changes as it swims around eating and being a tadpole.

The change starts when the tadpole begins to grow hind legs. The hind legs start out tiny, then grow bigger and bigger. After the hind legs grow, the front legs appear.

The front legs have been growing underneath the skin and, when they are ready, they pop out fully formed. When the front legs pop out, the tail starts to shrink back into the body. Then a mouth, sometimes with teeth, forms! The gills disappear and lungs form so that the frog can live on land. The tadpole is now ready to be an adult frog.

9.5 The End: Adult Frogs

The adult frog looks very different from the tadpole. It can sit and hop and move around on the land. It has lungs to breathe air, and it has eyes and even a kind of ear to hear sounds. The adult frog doesn't have to eat algae, but has a long, sticky tongue to catch flies.

There are lots of different kinds of frogs. There are Leopard Frogs that have strong legs for jumping. And there are African Clawed Frogs that have claws on their hind feet.

Frogs can also be different colors. There are green frogs and brown frogs and blue frogs and red frogs and yellow frogs. The banana frog is pale green and yellow and has funny looking feet used for climbing.

9.6 Summary

○ Frog eggs have a soft outer goo that sticks them together.

○ A tadpole starts to change into a frog when the hind legs grow.

○ Adult frogs come in different sizes and colors.

Chapter 10 Our Balanced Earth

10.1 In the Balance

If you go outside early in the morning, you might see a hummingbird getting nectar from a flower. You might also notice the flower growing from the soil. In the soil, you might see bugs crawling around finding food. You might notice the water from the rain pooled around the base of the flower and bugs drinking from the pool. You might think about the little protists swimming in the pool of water. You might also notice the Sun feeding the flower and feeding the protists in the water—the water that bugs are drinking and the flower is using to make nectar for the hummingbird. And now you notice you are all the way back to thinking about the hummingbird!

On Earth, all of the creatures are in some way connected to each other. The water and the air and the Sun are also connected to all the plants and animals. Also, everything on Earth is delicately balanced. There is just enough water, just enough oxygen, just enough nitrogen, just enough of everything in the right balance so that life can thrive on Earth.

10.2 Keeping the Balance

What does it take to keep the balance? If you close your eyes and stand on one foot, you can think about what it means to keep balanced. What do your hands do? Can you rest them against your sides, or do you need to put them out in the air? What is your foot on the ground doing? Can you feel it rock back and forth from side to side trying to keep your body upright? What happens when you start to tilt to one side? Do your arms go up or down in response? What about your other foot—can you feel it moving in the air to keep the balance? How does your body know when to move your arms or your legs to stay balanced?

Your body knows how to stay balanced because your body can tell your brain when you are beginning to lose your balance. And your brain can then tell your arms or legs to move so that you can go back to being balanced. This happens because your body can send information to your brain about changes in your balance. And your body has ways to move that information back to your foot or arms. This is a kind of cycle that helps you stay balanced. A cycle is any series of events that repeat themselves.

10.3 Cycles

There are different types of cycles. You learned about two life cycles—the life cycle of the butterfly and the life cycle of the frog. But there are other types of cycles too. There are water cycles and air cycles and food cycles. All of these cycles help keep water or air or food balanced on Earth so the Earth can stay balanced.

The food cycle works in the same way. Animals eat plants, and when the animals die, their molecules go into the ground helping new plants grow, and the new plants provide food for new animals.

Food Cycle

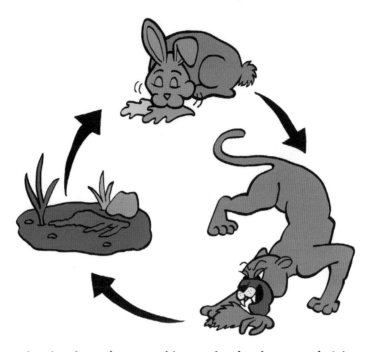

The air cycle helps keep the air balanced. You breathe in oxygen and exhale carbon dioxide. Plants breathe in carbon dioxide and exhale oxygen. And so the molecules of oxygen and carbon dioxide cycle back and forth between you and the plants around you!

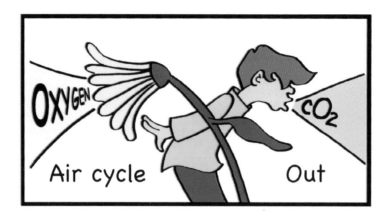

Water Cycle

The water cycle, cycles the water on Earth. You can watch the water cycle in your back yard. The rain brings pools of water, and the Sun heats the water which then evaporates back into the sky, where the rain will bring it down again.

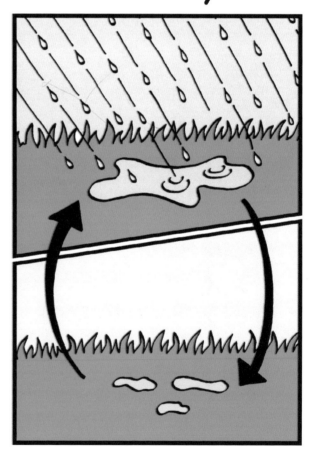

10.4 Summary

- The Earth is delicately balanced for life.

- A cycle is any set of events that repeat.

- There are different cycles that help keep the Earth balanced, such as the food cycle, the air cycle and the water cycle.